I0815520

FIRST WORDS IN...
French
français
père
mère
enfant
nourriture
by Kirsten Chang
BLASTOFF! READERS
1
BELLWETHER MEDIA • MINNEAPOLIS, MN

Blastoff! Readers are carefully developed by literacy experts to build reading stamina and move students toward fluency by combining standards-based content with developmentally appropriate text.

Level 1 provides the most support through repetition of high-frequency words, light text, predictable sentence patterns, and strong visual support.

Level 2 offers early readers a bit more challenge through varied sentences, increased text load, and text-supportive special features.

Level 3 advances early-fluent readers toward fluency through increased text load, less reliance on photos, advancing concepts, longer sentences, and more complex special features.

★ **Blastoff! Universe**

Reading Level

Grade K

Grades 1–3

Grade 4

This edition first published in 2026 by Bellwether Media, Inc.

Library of Congress Cataloging-in-Publication Data

LC record for French available at: https://lccn.loc.gov/2025018615

Editor: Suzane Nguyen Designer: Andrea Schneider

Printed in the United States of America, North Mankato, MN.

Table of Contents

Bonjour!

I am Alma. *Bonjour!* That is hello in French, or *français*.

Words to Know

- bonsoir (bon-SWAH) .... good evening
- je m'appelle (zhuh ma-PELL) .... my name is
- oui (WEE) .... yes
- non (NOHN) .... no
- s'il vous plaît (seel voo PLAY)...... please
- au revoir (oh reh-VWAH)........... goodbye
- français (FRAHN-say)................. French

bonjour (bon-JOOR)
hello

Millions of people speak French. It is spoken on four **continents**!

French-speaking Countries

At Home

Louis lives in a *maison*. He lives with his *famille*.

Words to Know

- maison (may-ZON) .... house
- famille (fam-EE) .... family
- mère (MARE) .... mother
- père (PARE) .... father
- frère (FRARE) .... brother
- sœur (souhr) .... sister

sœur

frère

famille

Charlotte plays with *jouets* in her *chambre*.

Words to Know

- chambre (SHAHM-bruh) .... bedroom
- jouets (ZHOO-way) .... toys
- lampe (lomp) .... lamp
- affiche (ah-FEESH) .... poster
- placard (PLEH-carr) .... closet

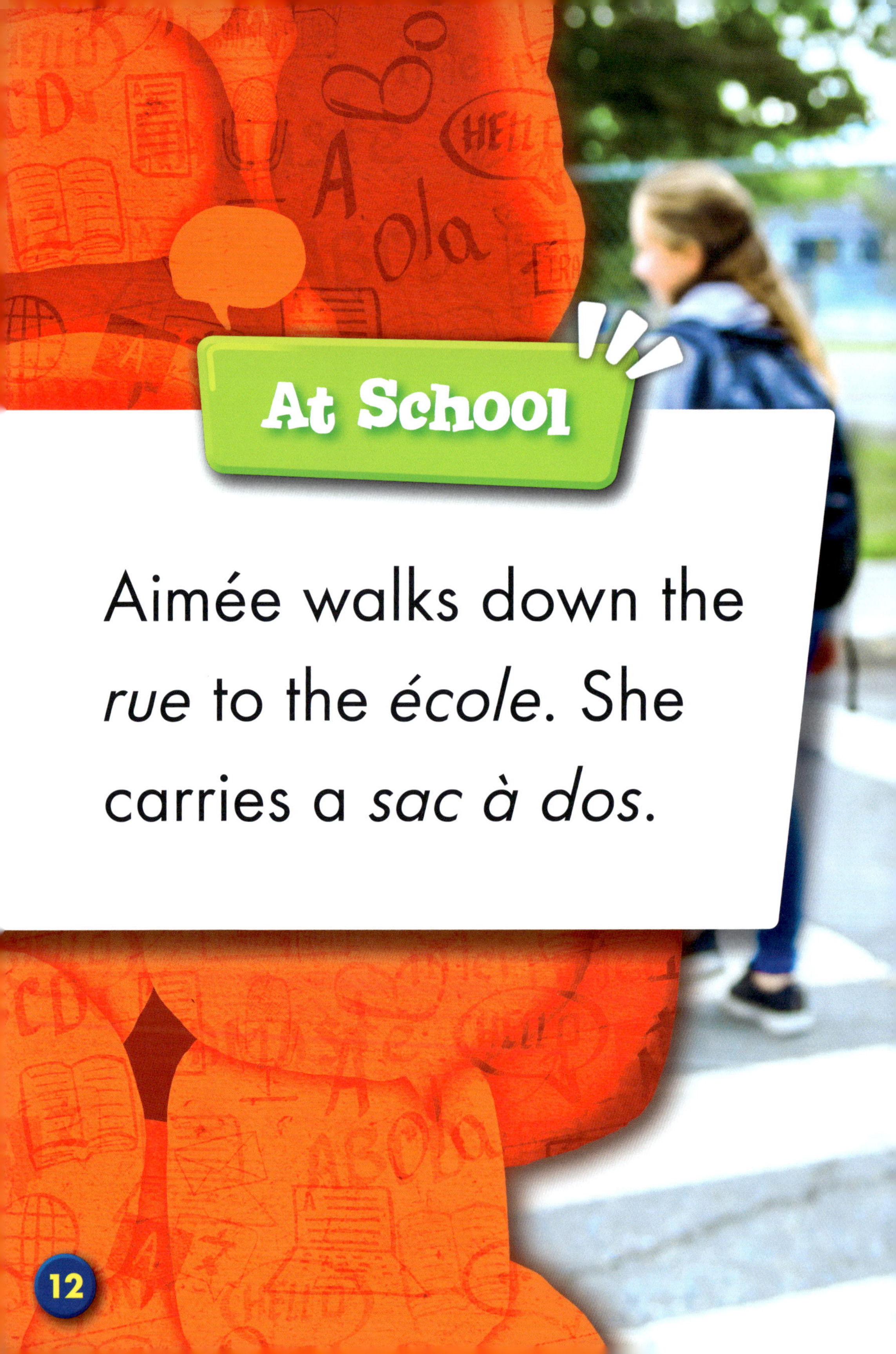

At School

Aimée walks down the *rue* to the *école*. She carries a *sac à dos*.

Words to Know

- école (ay-KOLE) .... school
- rue (ROO) .... street
- sac à dos (sack ah DOO) .... backpack
- maître (may-truh).......... teacher (male)
- maîtresse (may-TRESS) ....
  .... teacher (female)

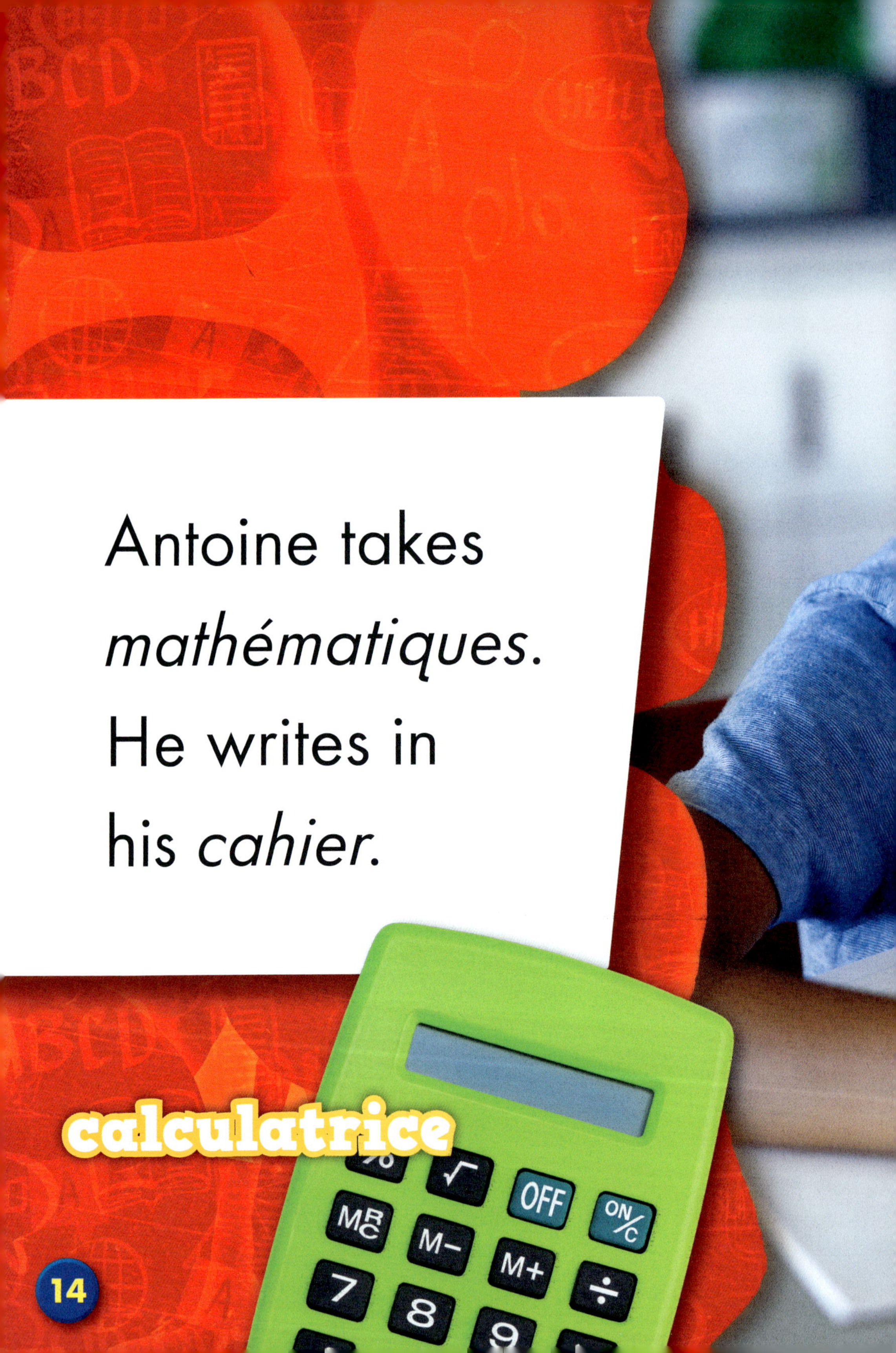

Antoine takes *mathématiques.* He writes in his *cahier.*

Count in French
un (euhn).......... 1
deux (deuh)........... 2
trois (twah)... 3
quatre (kat).......... 4
cinq (sank)...... 5
six (seese).............. 6
sept (set).......... 7
huit (weet)............ 8
neuf (nuhf)..... 9
dix (deese).......... 10
crayon
Words to Know
• cours (COOR)....................................course
• mathématiques (MAT-eh-mat-EEK)..math
• calculatrice (cal-cue-la-TREESE)...calculator
• crayon (cray-ON)............................pencil
• cahier (kai-YAY).............................notebook
• pupitre (pyoo-PI-truh).......................desk

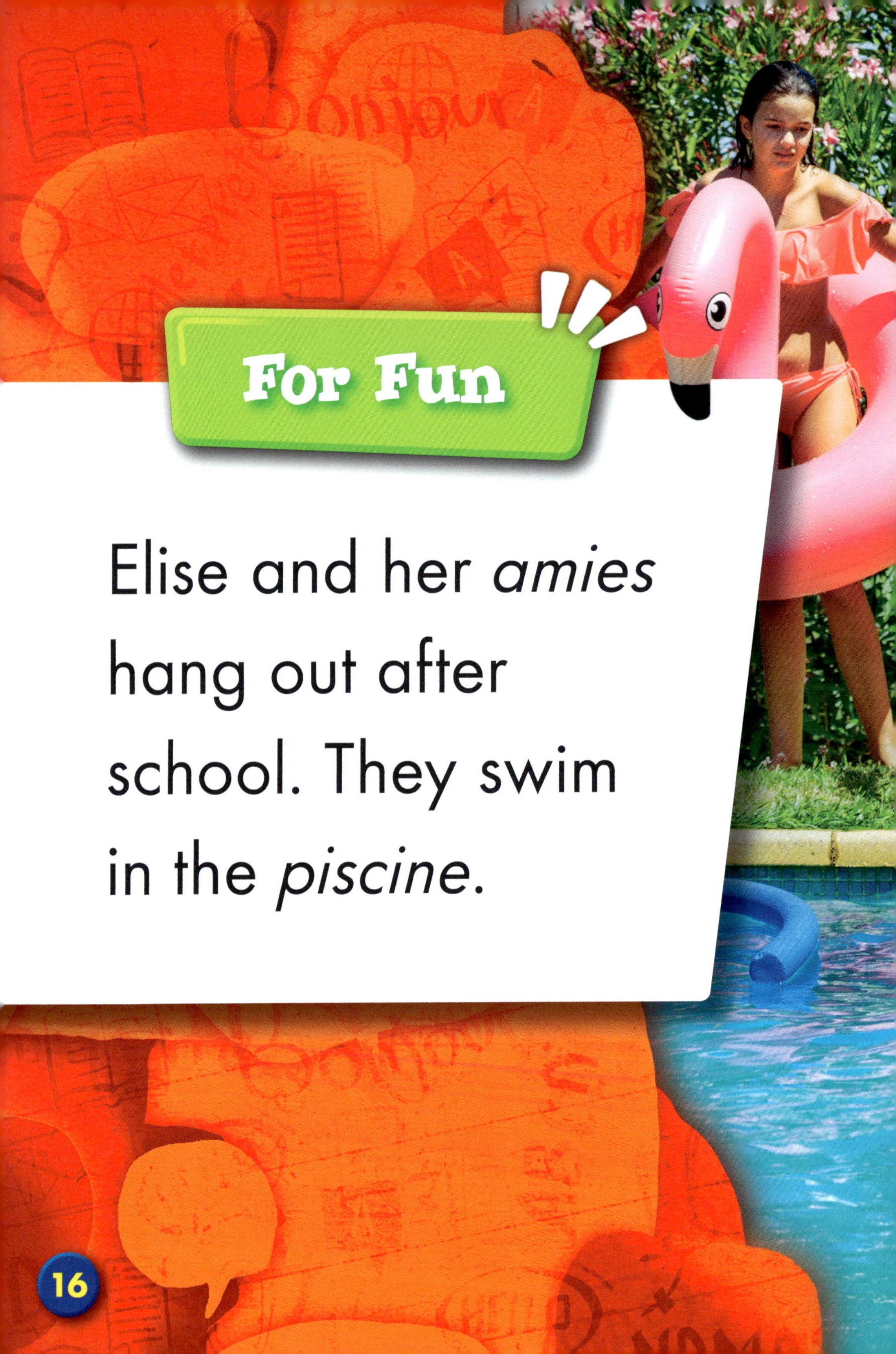

For Fun

Elise and her *amies* hang out after school. They swim in the *piscine*.

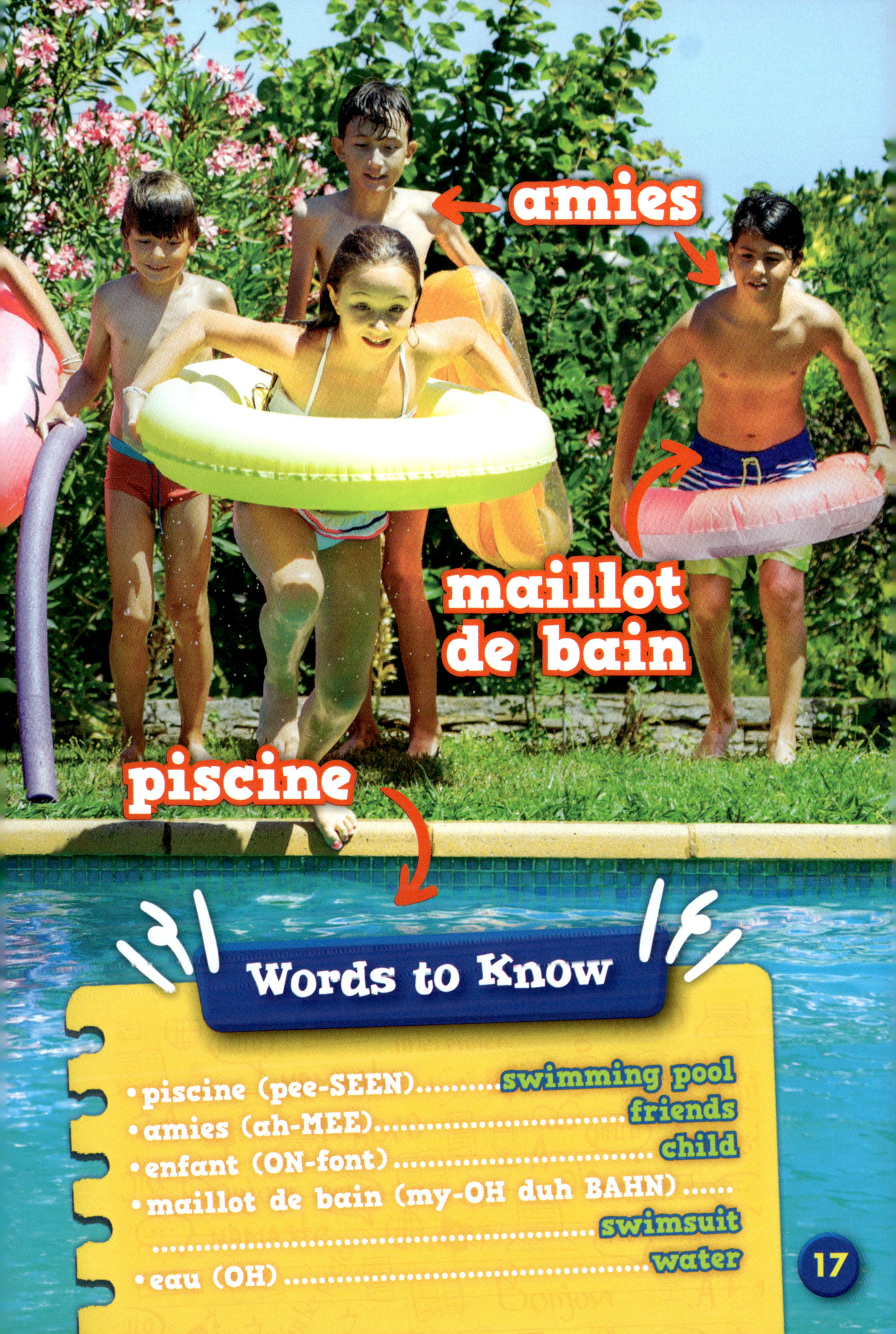

Words to Know

- piscine (pee-SEEN)........swimming pool
- amies (ah-MEE)........friends
- enfant (ON-font)........child
- maillot de bain (my-OH duh BAHN)........swimsuit
- eau (OH)........water

Gabriel eats *dîner*.
There is *pain*
and *fromage*.
Crème brûlée
is a treat!

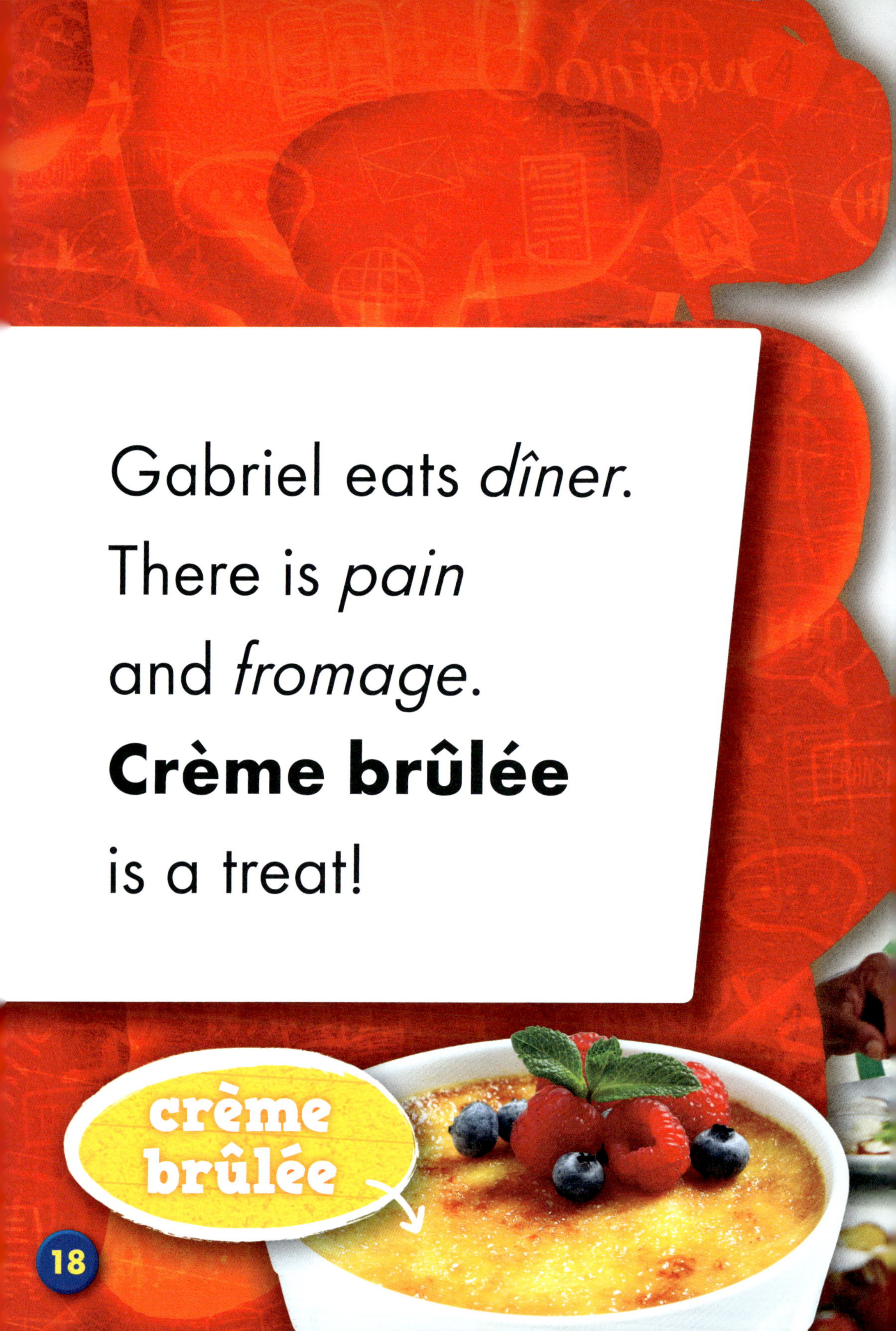

Words to Know

- dîner (deen-AY) .... dinner
- nourriture (noo-REE-toor) .... food
- pain (PAHN) .... bread
- fromage (fro-MAHJ) .... cheese
- assiette (ahs-YET) .... plate
- fourchette (for-SHET) .... fork
- tasse (TASS) .... cup

Bonne Nuit!

Rose puts on *pyjamas*.
Time for *lit*! *Bonne nuit*!

Words to Know

- pyjamas (pee-ZHA-ma) .... pajamas
- livres (LEEV-ruh) .... books
- couverture (coo-vare-TURE) .... blanket
- lit (LEE) .... bed
- merci (mare-SEE) .... thank you
- au revoir (OOH reh-vwah) .... bye

Glossary

continents

very large areas of land; there are seven continents on Earth.

crème brûlée

a sweet custard with a hard sugar top

To Learn More

AT THE LIBRARY

Corral, Jacy. *My First French Words*. San Antonio, Tex.: Modern Kid Press, 2024.

Golkar, Golriz. *See and Say French*. North Mankato, Minn.: Capstone, 2025.

Murray, Julie. *France*. Minneapolis, Minn.: Abdo Kids, 2025.

ON THE WEB

FACTSURFER

Factsurfer.com gives you a safe, fun way to find more information.

1. Go to www.factsurfer.com.
2. Enter "French" into the search box and click 🔍.
3. Select your book cover to see a list of related content.

Index

The images in this book are reproduced through the courtesy of: Jacob Lund, front cover; Brad Pict, p. 3; Rido, pp. 4-5; MisterStock, p. 6 (continent); FamVeld, pp. 6-7; famveldman, pp. 8-9; 24Novembers, p. 10 (lampe); SolStock, pp. 10-11; Louis-Photo, pp. 12-13; BetterStock, p. 14 (calculatrice); wavebreak3, pp. 14-15; Sergey Novikov, pp. 16-17; New Africa, p. 18 (crème brûlée); monkeybusinessimages, pp. 18-19; CHUYN, p. 20 (livres); Sergii Mostovyi, pp. 20-21; FrankRamspott/ Getty Images, p. 22 (continents); M.studio, p. 22 (crème brûlée).